Collections for Young Scholars™

Phonics Review
Activity Sheets

PROGRAM AUTHORS
Marilyn Jager Adams
Carl Bereiter
Jan Hirshberg
Valerie Anderson

CONSULTING AUTHORS
Michael Pressley
Marsha Roit
Iva Carruthers
Bill Pinkney

OPEN COURT PUBLISHING COMPANY

Cover art by Nelle Davis
Illustrated by Jack Wallen

Printed in the United States of America

ISBN 0–8126–2238–3

10 9 8 7 6 5

Contents

Choose the sentence that tells about the picture. Write it on the line.

1. (Nap on a mat.)
   Nat on a man.

_____

2. The man has a ham.
   (The man has a hat.)

_____

3. Pam pats the pan.
   (Pam pats the hat.)

_____

4. Hap sat in a pat.
   Hap sat in a pan.

_____

5. Sam has a hat.
   Sam has a mat.

_____

Name

Fill in a word to complete each rhyme.

Then complete the picture to go with the rhyme.

1. Sam is a man.

   His hat is _____.

2. Pam sat

   on a _____.

3. Here I am

   with Sam and _____.

4. Ann and Hap

   look at the _____.

Name

Choose the sentence that tells about the picture. Write it on the line.

1. The pen is on the bed.
   The pet is on the bed.

_____

2. Ten hens are in the nest.
   Ten hams are in the nest.

_____

3. Dad has a nap.
   Dad has a net.

_____

4. Ben mends the dent.
   Ben mends the tent.

_____

5. Ted has ham in a pan.
   Ted has ham in a pen.

_____

Name

Fill in the words to complete each sentence.

1.  bed

   let

   I _____ this pet

   nap on the _____.

2. hen

   nest

   The _____ is on her

   _____.

3. ham

   pan

   Ben has _____

   in the _____.

4. bed

   pen

   Peg's _____ is on

   the _____.

5. ten

   mend

   Ted has _____ tacks

   to _____ the map.

Write *a* or *e* in each blank to complete the words.
Then draw a picture to go with the sentences.

1. Tab is Ann's pet c___t.

   Tab n___ps on a t___n mat.

   Tab naps b___st on Ann's l___p.

2. Pam has a pet h___n.

   The h___n p___cks on a ham.

   Then it n___ps on Pam's b___d.

3. Jack has a c___p for Dad.

   The c___p is bl___ck and tan.

   It has D___d on it.

Name

Read each sentence. Choose the correct picture and
draw the missing part.

Name

1. A black pen is on the desk.

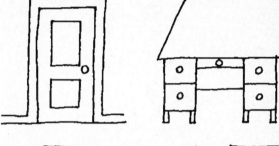

2. The bed has a pet on it.

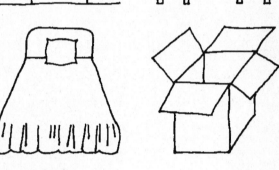

3. A cat sat on the man's lap.

4. The nest has a hen.

5. Set the can in the pan.

Choose the sentence that tells about the picture.
Write the sentence on the line.

1. Tim sticks a pin in the mat.
   Tim sticks a pin in the map.
   Tim pins a stick in the map.

_____

2. Kim will fill the big sack.
   Kim will rip the big snack.
   Kim lifts the sack onto her back.

_____

3. The hill slid on Jack and Jill.
   Jack and Jill fell on the hill.
   Jack and Jill slid on the hill.

_____

4. Jim lifts the kitten from the hat.
   The kitten lifts Jim from the hat.
   The kitten lifts the hat for Jim.

_____

5. Ten rabbits and a pig sit on a hill.
   Some pigs and a rabbit sit on a hill.
   Seven pigs and ten rabbits sit on a hill.

_____

Name

Choose the word that best completes each sentence.

1. You can pet a _____.   pig   pin

2. Mend a rip with a _____.   pin   nip

3. Fill a _____.   big   bag

4. A hand can be a _____.   fist   fast

5. A glass can _____.   tip   pit

6. A pan has a _____.   lit   lid

7. If you are ill, you are _____. sack   sick

8. If a glass tips, the milk will _____.   spill   spell

9. A twig is a _____.   stick   stack

10. Camp in a _____.   tint   tent

11. The sled slid on the _____.   fill   hill

12. If you win, you did the _____. nest   best

13. The hat has a _____.   brim   whim

Choose the sentence that tells about the picture.
Write the sentence on the line.

1.

A rock sits on the frog.

The frog sits on a rock.

The frog sits on a log.

2.

Six rabbits hop to the top of the hill.

The big rabbit hops in front.

Two rabbits hop to the top of the hill.

3.

Todd's dog is next to the cot.

Todd's dog is on top of the cot.

The cot is on Todd's dog.

4.

Mom drops Bob's pot.

Bob's mom drops a pot.

Bob drops Mom's pot.

5.

Tom stops to toss a rock at the pond.

Tom stops to toss the pond.

A rock in the pond stops Tom.

Name

Fill in the words to complete each sentence.

1.  top

    dog

    We will jog with our _____ to

    the _____ of the hill.

2.  socks

    knock

    Did you _____ his two

    _____ off the dock?

3.  spots

    frog

    What did the _____ tell the

    dog with black _____?

4.  fox

    rocks

    The _____ will hop on

    the _____.

5.  box

    dolls

    Meg put six _____ into

    a _____.

Phonics Review

Read each sentence. Choose the correct picture and
draw the missing part.

1. The big pot has a red spot.

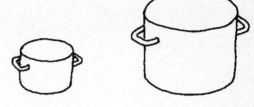

2. The rat ran up the ramp.

3. The pet has spots.

4. The sock has six dots.

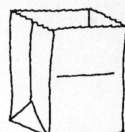

5. Fill the box with pickles.

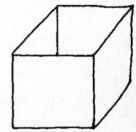

Name

Write *i* or *o* in each blank to complete the words.

Then draw a picture to go with the sentences.

1. Todd has a b____g box.

   S____x rocks are in the b____x.

   Todd drops his box of r____cks.

   He knocks the t____p off the

   b____x.

   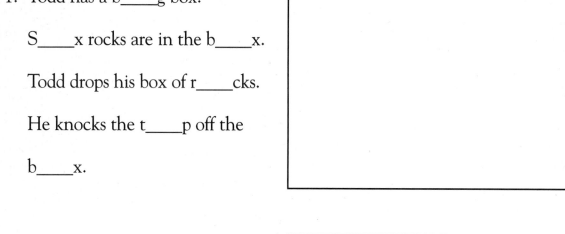

2. Six fr____gs are at the pond.

   The frogs s____t on a big l____g.

   A big f____x stops by the l____g.

   The s____x frogs h____p into the

   p____nd.

3. Skip is Tim's d____g.

   Skip d____gs in the grass.

   T____m's dad spots Sk____p.

   "St____p, Skip!" says Dad.

   Skip st____ps. He l____cks Dad's

   hand.

Choose the word that best completes each sentence.

1. An ant is a _____.   bus   bug

2. Bananas are in a _____.   bunch   bump

3. The cat slept on the _____.   rub   rug

4. A hot dog is on a _____.   bun   bin

5. I will wrap the mug in a _____.   cluck   cloth

6. I giggle when I have _____.   fun   fan

7. The man has a dump _____.   trick   truck

8. Have a bath in a _____.   tub   tug

9. The _____ kept us hot.   sub   sun

10. You can hit a _____.   drum   drab

11. Drink from a _____.   cup   cut

12. I have a pet _____.   dusk   duck

13. Chuck has a sandwich for _____.   lunch   lump

14. A camel has a _____.   hunt   hump

Choose the sentence that tells about the picture.
Write the sentence on the line.

1. The kids run to the bus.
   Six kids miss the bus.
   The kids sit in the bus.

_____

2. Gus is stuck in the mud.
   Mud stuck to the truck.
   Gus dumps a bucket of mud.

_____

3. The dog hid from the sun.
   The dog runs in the sun.
   The dog naps in the hot sun.

_____

4. A branch is on the bug.
   A bunch of bugs sit on the branch.
   A bug is on the branch.

_____

5. A pig digs in the mud.
   Some mud dug up a pig.
   The pig had mud for lunch.

_____

Choose the word to complete each sentence.
Write the word on the line.

1. If it has legs, it must be a _____.   bag   bug   rug

2. If it has buds, it must be a _____.   plant   lump   plump

3. If it has milk in it, it must be a _____.   cut   cot   cup

4. If it can hop, it must be a _____.   fog   frog   fig

5. If it has a hot dog, it must be a _____.   bump   bunt   bun

6. If it has a shell, it must be a _____.   crash   crab   crunch

7. If it is a little bit wet, it must be _____.   dump   damp   bump

8. If it is on a camel, it must be a _____.   camp   hump   dump

9. If it hunts rabbits, it must be a _____.   fox   box   fix

10. If it can fix a rip, it must be a _____.   path   punch   patch

11. If it can swim, it must be a _____.   dusk   duck   deck

12. If it catches fish, it must be a _____.   net   nest   nut

13. If it crunches, it must be _____.   crisp   cost   cub

14. When you giggle, you have _____.   fan   fund   fun

Name

Read each hint. Fill in the vowel to complete the word.

1. A pet   c___t

2. A big scratch   c___t

3. A camp bed   c___t

4. It says tick-tock   cl___ck

5. A switch says _____   cl___ck

6. What a hen says   cl___ck

7. Put things in this   b___g

8. Something that is not little   b___g

9. An insect   b___g

10. Something you cannot find is _____   l___st

11. The one at the end   l___st

12. A _____ of things to do   l___st

13. A little branch   st___ck

14. Trapped in mud   st___ck

15. _____ the blocks   St___ck

Name

Choose the word that completes each sentence.
Write the words on the lines.

1. Phil has pigs on his _____.   barn

   His animals live in a _____.   farm

   car

2. It is _____ at the park.   yarns

   I can see lots of _____.   dark

   stars

3. Carla got into her _____.   start

   It was hard to _____.   card

   car

4. Marsha and her pals had a _____.   spark

   They ran to catch bubbles in the   yard

   _____.   party

5. Charles is an _____.   jar

   He has his brushes in a _____.   art

   artist

Name

Read each sentence. Choose the correct picture and
draw the missing part.

Name

1. The gerbil has a kernel of corn.

2. The shirt has a circle of dirt.

3. A turtle is in the first box.

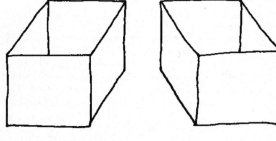

4. Her purse is purple.

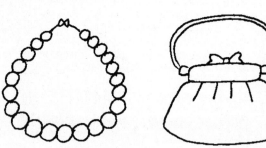

5. A farmer is by the turkey.

Phonics Review

Read the sentences. Color and add the things that are missing to make the picture match the sentences.

This is a farm with a red barn.

A garden is by the bird bath.

A girl picks peppers at the edge of the garden.

She has a large basket of peppers.

A black bird is on the hedge.

A dog barks at the bird.

A cat curls up in the grass next to the garden.

The farmer is by the barn.

He has on a purple shirt with a zipper.

He has a smudge of dirt on his arm.

Name

Read the word in the box. Then read the sentence.
Change the word in the box to make a new rhyming
word that will complete the sentence.

1. | card | Not soft is _____.

2. | charmer | The person who runs a farm is a _____.

3. | burn | _____ the knob to open the box.

4. | shirt | Some bugs live in the _____.

5. | rammer | Hit a tack with a _____.

6. | car | The cut on his leg left a _____.

7. | charger | My truck is large. Your truck is _____.

8. | swirls | The kids with red shirts are _____.

9. | thirst | If I start, I will be _____.

10. | fatter | The person who bats is the _____.

11. | starkest | The kitchen is the _____ part of the cottage.

12. | bark | This big fish can hurt you. It is a _____.

13. | star | Jam comes in a _____.

14. | purse | A person who helps when you are sick is a _____.

15. | barn | Mom knits a scarf with _____.

Choose the sentence that tells about the picture.
Write the sentence on the line.

1. Jake can rake a cake.
   Jake can bake a cake.
   Jake can bake a cave.

_____

2. The plate is on the grapes.
   The plate has ten grapes.
   The grapes are on the plate.

_____

3. The snake is in a cage.
   The snake is in a cave.
   The snake is in a race.

_____

4. A spaceman saves the plane.
   The plane made a trip to space.
   The place made a trip to plane.

_____

5. Kate's name is on the plate.
   Jake's name is on the page.
   Kate's name is on the page.

_____

Use the letters in the box and the word ending below it to make a word to complete each sentence.

tr	d	str	pl	st

_____ ay

1. Kate can go, but James must _____.

2. It's a hot summer _____.

3. We kept the _____ kitten.

4. Place the dishes on a _____.

5. Will you _____ tag with me?

sn	m	tr	t	s

_____ ail

6. Letters come in the _____.

7. An animal with a shell is a _____.

8. A ship can have a _____.

9. My dog wags its _____.

10. We can skate along a _____.

Copyright © 1996 Open Court Publishing Company

Phonics Review

Choose the word to complete each sentence.

Write the word on the line.

1. If it is fixing a rip, it must be _____.   tap   tape

2. If you run fast, you must be in a _____.   rack   race

3. If it is made of glass, it must be a _____.   pan   pane

4. If it hurts, it must be a _____.   pan   pain

5. If it kept the sun from your face,

   it must be a _____.   cap   cape

6. If it is not Mom, it must be _____.   Dad   day

7. If it is a rocket, it can blast into _____.   spats   space

8. If it makes you think, it must be

   your _____.   bran   brain

9. If a dog wagged it, it must be a _____.   tag   tail

10. If you can tell it, it must be a _____.   tack   tale

11. If it can catch bugs, it must be a _____.   trap   tray

12. If you are playing, it must be a _____.   gram   game

13. If it can slither, it must be a _____.   snack   snake

14. If it is pinned to a shirt, it must be a _____.   badge   bag

Name

Choose the word to complete each sentence.
Write the word on the line.

1. A car has four _____.   wheels   whales

2. You must not tell a _____.   second   secret

3. A number is _____.   three   the

4. An insect with a stinger is a _____. bee   beet

5. When two things are the same size,

   they are _____.   even   evil

6. Plant a _____.   seep   seed

7. _____ is a girl.   She   Shed

8. _____ in a bed.   Sleep   Sled

9. Tell _____ your name.   met   me

10. Socks fit on your _____.   fat   feet

11. Glasses can help a person _____.   seed   see

12. The part of a shirt that covers your arm

    is the _____.   sleeve   slave

13. A shark has sharp _____.   teen   teeth

14. A person who saves others is a _____. helmet   hero

Choose the sentence that tells about the picture.
Write the sentence on the line.

1. Pete has bare feet.
   Pete has bare feast.
   Pete has three feet.

_____

2. Steve eats green beads.
   Steve eats green bees.
   Steve eats green beans.

_____

3. Neal eats thirteen peaches.
   The peach bit Neal.
   Neal eats a sweet peach.

_____

4. The tree has lost its leaves.
   The tree has lots of leaves.
   The leaves fell off the tree.

_____

5. The seal eats meat.
   The seal eats three fish in the sea.
   The seal does a trick for a treat.

_____

6. Eve marks one weed.
   Eve marks one week.
   Eve marks three weaks.

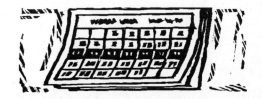

_____

Name

Choose the word that completes each sentence.
Write the word on the line.

1. It was a _____ day. Jenny ran to the

        sunny   sorry

_____ to pick a bunch of _____.

  felt   field   daisies   days

She put the _____ in a _____.

        daisies   days   jolly   jar

2. A_____ of _____ is in the yard.

   family   funny   rusty   rabbits

There are three _____. The mommy and the

        babies   buggies

_____ stay near the _____.

  daddy   doggy   puppies   bunnies

3. I can read this _____. It has a prince and a

       study   story

_____ king. It has a _____ ending.

  silly   sixty   happy   hay

I will read other _____ like this one.

    ladies   stories

Choose the word that completes each sentence.
Write the word on the line.

1. We can _____ a story.	read red real
2. You can sleep in a _____.	red bead bed
3. Mom cut a _____ of cake.	peek piece peck
4. The wagon is missing a _____.	weed well wheel
5. Honey made my fingers _____.	happy sticky steamy
6. This is the _____ peach I ever ate.	beast bets best
7. I want to do a _____ job next week.	beater better beady
8. The _____ cat takes a nap.	sloppy sleepy slappy
9. The farmer plants wheat in this _____.	field felt feed
10. Baby birds eat seeds at the bird _____.	fever feeder fed

Name

Choose the words that answer each question.
Write the words on the lines.

1. What has a tail? _____ _____ _____	puppy bunny penny sheep
2. What comes from a tree? _____ _____ _____	leaf peach seed feet
3. What can you eat? _____ _____ _____	meat pennies cookies jelly
4. Which are people? _____ _____ _____	teacher meter ladies men
5. What comes from the sea? _____ _____ _____	seals seaweed jets shells
6. Which have beaks? _____ _____ _____	guppies geese eagles hens

Use the letters in the box and the word ending below it to make a word to complete each sentence.

h	b		l

_____ike

1. I _____ apple pie, but Bill likes cherry.

2. The girls went for a _____ at the park.

3. Don't forget your helmet when you ride your _____.

h	sl		r

_____ide

4. I like to _____ on ice.

5. Mike wants to _____ a pony.

6. The rabbit needs to _____ from the fox.

p	tw	sh

_____ine

7. The forest had large _____ trees.

8. Did you tie the package with _____?

9. A candle can _____ in the dark.

Name

Read each sentence. Choose the word that will complete
the sentence. Write the word on the line.

1. Sam _____ his wet feet.
        dry   dries   drips

2. Mom and Dad _____ chicken for dinner.
        fry   free   fries

3. Let's _____ a kite.
        by   fly   flip

4. Some _____ cry when they are hungry.
        bubbles   babies   buggies

5. The furry _____ plays all night long.
        spy   penny   puppy

6. Each child _____ very hard to finish.
        tried   trays   trips

7 My tummy hurts from eating too many _____.
        pipes   ties   pies

8. The bird _____ high in the sky.
        tries   flies   flakes

Name

Read each sentence. Pick the word that makes sense
in the sentence and write the word on the line.

Mike is a brave _____. He is a mighty dragon

        knit   knight

_____.

  fighter   fitter

Today, Mike _____ off to fight a dragon. But this dragon

        rids   rides

does not _____ to fight. It likes to _____ in its

     lick   like   sit   sight

cave and _____ on fine food.

     din   dine

Mike says, "Dragon, come here in the_____.

                         lit   light

I am here to fight you."

"I will not fight," says the dragon. "Fighting is not

_____. Come and _____ with me."

  rit   right   din   dine

So Mike and the dragon dine. "This dinner is _____ for

                       fit   fight

a king!" sighs Mike.

"Oh it's better than that," says the dragon. "It's fit for a dragon.

Here, have a _____ of pie."

     slick   slice

Name

Read the word in the box. Then read the sentence.
Change the word in the box to make a new rhyming
word to complete the sentence.

1. | try | The opposite of *wet* is _____.

2. | pie | You must not tell a _____.

3. | tight | The opposite of *day* is _____.

4. | tie | Bake cherries in a _____.

5. | rice | You can slip and slide on slick _____.

6. | cried | The wet shirts _____ in the summer breeze.

7. | line | When something belongs to me, it is _____.

8. | write | Danny takes a _____ of peach pie.

9. | cry | Planes fly in the _____.

10. | night | The opposite of *wrong* is _____.

11. | sight | The opposite of *dark* is _____.

12. | dine | Plant nine fine _____ trees in a city park.

13. | fries | The bird family _____ high.

14. | by | The little puppies _____ for their mother.

15. | spied | The bunny _____ to get into the garden.

Read the sentence. Choose the word that completes the sentence. Write the word on the blank line.

1. If my sock has a hole, I can wiggle my _____.

goes   toes   tops

2. When my dog has a _____, he digs a hole for it.

tone   bond   bone

3. The forest is a safe home for a _____.

doe   hoe   dome

4. Joe _____ a long note to Tom.

robe   wrote   wrong

5. The phone on the desk _____ ring, ring, ring.

goes   globe   hoes

6. The funny _____ made us giggle.

spoke   job   joke

7. King Moe wore a velvet _____ and sat

rob   robe   rose

on a stone _____.

throne   toes   tone

Name

Read the word in the box. Then read the sentence.
Change the word in the box to make a new rhyming
word to complete the sentence.

1. | goat | You can ride on a lake in a _____.

2. | road | An animal that looks like a frog is a _____.

3. | croak | A tree that comes from an acorn is an _____.

4. | so | It's time to start. Let's _____!

5. | soars | You can paddle a boat with _____.

6. | go | The opposite of *yes* is _____.

7. | coat | An animal with a beard is a billy _____.

8. | oar | A lion makes a mighty _____.

9. | moat | When something does not sink, it can _____.

10. | clover | The opposite of *under* is _____.

11. | roach | A person who helps a team is a _____.

12. | roast | In the morning you can eat _____.

13. | stony | A little horse is a _____.

14. | load | Cars drive on a _____.

Name

Read the sentences. Then draw the things that are missing to make the picture match the sentences.

The sink is full of soap suds.

There is a window over the sink.

It is snowing. Snowflakes float past the window.

A pot is on the stove.

A bowl of popcorn is on the table. The bowl is yellow.

Name

Choose the word to complete each sentence.

Write the word on the line.

1. If it floats on a lake, it must be a _____.	bond boat bone
2. If you can sleep on it, it must be a _____.	cot coast cope
3. If it comes from the sky, it must be _____.	stone snob snow
4. If it's in a bowl, it must be _____.	opera oatmeal over
5. If it is on a stove, it must be a _____.	pot pond pole
6. If it rings, it must be a _____.	photo phone photograph
7. If it cleans your hands, it must be _____.	sop sow soap
8. If it ties things, it must be _____.	rob robe rope
9. If it runs in the forest, it must be a _____.	doe dose dome
10. If you can wiggle them, they must be _____.	tow toes toss

Phonics Review

The words in the box belong in the puzzle. Read the
clues to find where to write the words in the puzzle.

bugle	music	cute	united	pupil
cube	humor	huge	uniform	mule

ACROSS:

2. Very, very large

4. A fire fighter dresses in a

    ____.

7. Stars are on the flag of the

    ____ States.

8. A ____ is a musical instrument.

9. A block of ice is an ice ____.

DOWN:

1. A student

2. Something that is funny has

    ____.

3. Little kittens are soft and ____.

5. An animal that is like a horse

6. A band can play ____.

Name

Choose a word from the box that makes sense
in the sentence. Write the word on the line.

1. Mary is in a band.

   She likes to play _____.

   When it is her turn to play, the conductor

   will nod. That is her _____ to start.

cue
cut
music

2. Dad is driving the car.

   It has been a long trip.

   There are only a _____ miles left to go.

   He hopes he has the _____ he needs.

few
fuel
fund

3. Pat and Mike don't get along .

   All they do is _____.

   If Pat says the day is nice, Mike says it is

   too hot.

   They will use any _____ to fuss.

rescue
argue
excuse

4. Dad grilled this meat on the _____.

   He must have left it on too long.

   It's almost black, and it's hard to

   _____.

nephew
chew
barbecue

Choose the word that completes each sentence.
Write the word on the line.

1.
| cut |
| cube |
| cute |

Peg _____ a pink ribbon.

She tied it on her _____ kitten.

2.
| cub |
| cube |
| cue |

The keeper tossed a _____ of meat.

It landed by the lion _____ .

3.
| fuel |
| fun |
| few |

Just a _____ children can play.

We will have lots of _____ anyway.

4.
| cup |
| cue |
| cute |

Dad dropped his _____ .

That was a _____ for the cat to jump.

5.
| muddy |
| musty |
| music |

The marching band played _____ .

The players got _____ in the rain.

6.
| full |
| fuel |
| fell |

If we run out of _____ , the motor will quit.

I'm glad the tank is _____ .

7.
| unite |
| underneath |
| uniform |

Sarah likes her new _____ .

But she still has her old shirt on _____ .

8.
| us |
| use |
| unit |

Quentin gave _____ that purple quilt.

We _____ it in winter.

Name

Read each sentence. Choose the word that makes sense in
the sentence. Write the word on the line.

Betty is a _____ in a marching band. She plays a
          drummer   duster

_____ drum that is on wheels. People can hear the
  hug   huge

_____ of the drum from far away. Then they
thump-thump   quack-quack

know that the _____ will start quickly. They
         muffin   music

quit what they are doing and _____ to hear the band.
            rush   refuse

A _____ of Betty's pals are in the band. Dan
    fun   few

plays the _____ , and Shelly plays the _____.
    bungle   bugle   trumpet   trusty

This year the band got new _____ with shiny
        underline   uniforms

brass _____. The hats are quite_____.
  buttons   butter   cut   cute

Betty can't wait _____ the next parade.
    until   unit

Phonics Review

Name

Write the letter or letters to complete each word.

Then draw a line to the meaning of the word.

Write **u** on each line:

1. st____dent •   • Something that is not a lie

2. tr____th •   • A very big horn

3. r____ler •   • A person who has a
                                         teacher

4. t____ba •   • This can tell how long
                                         something is.

Write **u** and **e** on the lines:

5. t____n____ •   • Squeeze this to make paste
                                         come out.

6. fl____t____ •   • Blow in this to make music.

7. J____n____ •   • This is a song

8. t____b____ •   • A month of the year

Write **ue** on each line:

9. cl____ •   • The color of the sky

10. tr____ •   • The opposite of *made-up*

11. gl____ •   • A hint

12. bl____ •   • This can stick things together.

Name

Read each clue. Choose the correct word and
write it on the line.

1. You use this to sweep. Is it a broom or a boom?

   _____

2. I am not old. Am I newt or new?

   _____

3. Animals live here. Is it a zoo or a zoom?

   _____

4. Use this to chew. Is it a tool or a tooth?

   _____

5. Blow this up and play with it. Is it a balloon or a baboon?

   _____

6. This might make you laugh. Is it a caboose or a cartoon?

   _____

7. These keep your feet dry. Are they boots or boons?

   _____

8. This is a tool to serve ice cream. Is it a stoop or a scoop?

   _____

9. A bird did this. Is it flew or few?

   _____

10. We sail a ship. Are we the crew or the chew?

   _____

Name

Choose a word from the box that makes sense
in the sentence. Write the word on the line.

1. Sue has a cone with two _____ of

   ice cream. Stu has his ice cream in a dish.

   He likes to eat it with a _____.

   | soon |
   | spoon |
   | scoops |

2. Did you see the silly circus band?

   The tallest player tooted the little _____.

   The shortest player had the big _____!

   | tuba |
   | tuna |
   | flute |

3. The _____ got up too late.

   He missed the bus.

   Now he will be late for _____.

   | student |
   | stupid |
   | school |

4. Pete is a lifeguard at the swimming _____.

   He gave a few swimming lessons, too.

   He hopes he will not need to _____

   any swimmers.

   | rescue |
   | pool |
   | barbecue |

Name

Read the sentences. Choose the word that makes
sense in each blank. Write the word on the line.

Sue needs new _____. Sue wants _____ boots, not

       booms   boots   cute   cube

ugly boots. She sees little red boots, but they are _____ tight.

                                                   tube   too

Next, she sees the big green boots, but they are too _____.

                                           loop   loose

At last she tries the _____ boots. They are a perfect fit!

       boom   blue

They are _____! Now Sue has cool _____

      cool   cube   news   new

blue boots to wear to _____.

      school   spool

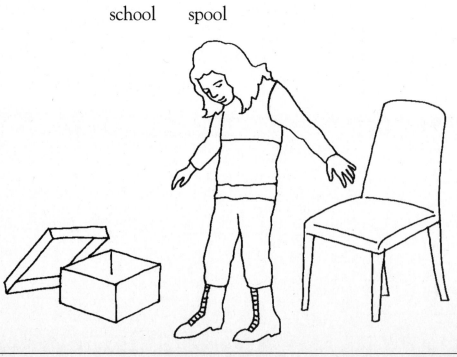

Name

Choose the word to complete each sentence.
Write the word on the line.

1. If it is candy, it must be _____.   sweet   swine

2. If it's a puppy, it must be _____.   cut   cute

3. If it's in the sky, it must be the _____.   moon   moan

4. If they have toes, they must be _____.   feet   fest

5. If it's a frog, it can _____.   hop   hoop

6. If it's a star, it can _____.   shin   shine

7. If you take a bath in it, it must be a

   _____.   tub   tube

8. If an actor stands on it, it must be a

   _____.   stag   stage

9. If it's a pet, it must be a _____.   bugle   beagle

10. If it grows on a tree, it must be a _____.   plum   plume

11. If you use it to scrub, it must be a _____.   sponge   spoon

12. If it makes music, it must be a _____.   boggle   bugle

13. If it's a high hill, it must be _____.   step   steep

14. If it's a map, it must be a _____.   glob   globe

15. If it's part of your leg, it must be your

   _____.   know   knee

Name

Add *-ed* or *-ing* to the word in the box to complete each sentence. Write the new word on the line.

1. Mandy is _____ at the ice rink.

   Last winter she _____ on the lake.

   skate

2. Yesterday Nat and Dave _____ on their bikes.

   Now they are _____ on skates.

   race

3. We _____ up the hill last night.

   Let's go _____ again next week.

   hike

4. Bill is _____ for a new game.

   He has _____ five dollars.

   save

5. Is this thunderstorm _____ you?

   Last night's storm sure _____ me!

   scare

6. This morning I _____ my snack with Phil.

   Now I am _____ my lunch with Sue.

   share

The chart has a place for a base word, the base word with the ending *-ed*, and the base word with the ending *-ing*. Fill in the missing words to complete the chart. Then use those words to complete the sentences.

Base word	Word + ed	Word + ing
zip	zipped	
	stopped	stopping
tape	taped	
snap		
plan		planning
	wiped	wiping

1. Kevin is _____ his fingers in time to the music.

2. The zipper is stuck. Shelly needs help _____ her jacket.

3. Please _____ your feet on the mat.

4. Yesterday we _____ what to bring to the picnic.

5. It's time to _____ playing.

6. The turtle _____ at a fly.

7. We are _____ the music from the band concert.

Name

Start with the word at the top of the box. Follow the directions for changing the word from line to line. Make new words to answer each question.

---

team

1. Add *s*. What comes from a tea kettle? _____

2. Add *r*. What is a little river? _____

3. Change *t* to *c*. What is a yell? _____

4. Take off *s*. What is thick milk? _____

5. Change *c* to *d*. What do you do when you sleep? _____

---

rip

6. Add *t*. What do you do when you stumble? _____

7. Add *s*. What is a long, narrow piece? _____

8. Add *e*. What is red or white on the flag? _____

9. Take off *st*. What kind of fruit is full-grown? _____

Add a word ending from the box to the beginning letters below it to make a word to complete each sentence. Write the word on the line.

ee	ow	ifty

thr_____

1. If you _____ a stick, the dog will fetch it.

2. A _____ person tries hard to save money.

3. The number after two is _____.

ink	eds	ug

shr_____

4. The puppy ripped the paper to _____.

5. This shirt is too big. I hope it will _____.

6. A _____ shows that you don't know.

atch	ape	ibble

scr_____

7. I like to _____ with my crayons.

8. The dog stopped to _____ an itch.

9. Dad had to _____ off the old paint.

Name

Choose the words that answer each question.
Write the words on the lines.

1. What can you hear? _____ _____ _____	scream squeak steep shriek
2. What can you do with water? _____ _____ _____	splash shred spray spill
3. What can grow? _____ _____ _____	shrub plant tree clever
4. What can you do with paper? _____ _____ _____	shrug scrunch scribble shred
5. What do you use for a meal? _____ _____ _____	spoon plate glass strike
6. Which can you eat? _____ _____ _____	spikes plums grapes cranberries

Phonics Review

Choose the letters to complete the words.
Write the letters on the lines.

Dear Pen Pal,

      I am writing from the middle of a f_____est. Camping is fun,
                               or   ear

but it's a lot of w_____k, too. The first thing we did was put up a tent.
              ar   or

I l_____ned that it is not smart to stand inside a tent until it's all
  or ear

the way up. It might fall on your h_____d!
                       ar   ea

      It rained last night. We h_____d the rain hit the tent. Today the
                         ar   ear

w_____ther is nice and w_____m. Dad and I will go fishing. He is
  ea ear   ar ea

digging for w_____ms to use as bait. Mom says catching fish is too
          ar or

h_____d. She and my sister w_____nt to go swimming inst_____d.
  ea ar   a ar   ea ar

Dad w_____ned them to stay in the shallow w_____ter.
   a ar   a ar

      I need to get r_____dy to fish. Don't w_____ry, I'll write again
             ear ea   a or

next week.

                                    Your pal,

                                   _____

Read the sentences. Decide which words from
the first sentence belong in each blank.
Write the words on the lines.

1. The birds have to work to get worms.

   They will take the _____ to the babies in the nest.

   Feeding the babies is hard _____.

2. Tim washed a dog to earn money.

   Then he will take the dog he _____ for a walk.

   Tim will _____ three dollars.

3. Mandy likes to watch her mom make bread.

   Mom lets Mandy put the _____ in a pan.

   Mandy can _____ Mom slice the warm _____.

4. The weather forecaster said we have a storm warning.

   That means we might have a big _____.

   It is not the best _____ for playing in the yard.

Select the word that answers the question.
Write the word on the line.

1. Which is stickier, water or honey? _____

2. Which is shinier, silver or paper? _____

3. Which is the warmest, a match, a furnace, or a candle? _____

4. Which is the tiniest, a moose, an ant, or a bird? _____

5. Which is the prickliest, a vine, a seed, or a cactus? _____

6. Which is faster, a turtle or a rabbit? _____

7. Which is the darkest, daytime, afternoon, or midnight? _____

8. Which is fluffier, a pillow or a cactus? _____

9. Which is sharper, a spoon or a knife? _____

10. Which is skinnier, a pencil or a log? _____

11. Which is the slowest, a fly, a snail, or a kitten? _____

12. Which is the jumpiest, a kangaroo, a snail, or a turtle? _____

13. Which is sweeter, cookies or cheese? _____

14. Which is the crunchiest, cheese, bananas, or carrots? _____

15. Which is brighter, lightning or a candle? _____

Add *-er* or *-est* to the underlined word in each sentence
to form a new word that will complete the sentence.
Write the new word on the line.
(Hint: Remember that some words change their spelling
before the ending is added.)

1. A candle is <u>hot</u>, but an oven is _____ than a candle.

2. A path is <u>wide</u>, but a street is _____ than a path.

3. A zebra is <u>heavy</u>, but an elephant is _____ than a zebra.

4. A peach is <u>tiny</u>, but a pea is _____ than a peach.

5. A horse is <u>fast</u>, a car is faster, but an airplane is the _____.

6. A pencil is <u>skinny</u>, a toothpick is skinnier, but thread is the
   _____ of all.

7. A raccoon is <u>little</u>, a chipmunk is _____ , but a butterfly is
   the _____ of all three.

8. A rose is <u>big</u>, a shrub is _____ , but a tree is the
   _____.

9. A stone is <u>light</u>, a twig is _____ , but a feather is the
   _____ of all.

Name

Read the first sentence. Change the underlined word
to make a word that will complete the second sentence.

1. We saw a <u>baby</u> rabbit.

   Three more _____ were in the nest.

2. The black kitten is <u>pretty</u>.

   The tan kitten is even _____.

3. We have to <u>hurry</u> to school.

   Yesterday we _____ , too.

4. Mom <u>worries</u> if I am late.

   She will _____ if I miss the bus.

5. Will you <u>watch</u> TV with me?

   I am _____ cartoons.

6. Stripe is a <u>friendly</u> dog.

   I think he's the _____ dog I know.

7. Shandra <u>emptied</u> the box.

   Then she put the _____ box on the shelf.

8. Warren is <u>teaching</u> me to paint.

   He is a good _____.

Read the word in the box. Then read the sentence.
Change the word in the box to make a new rhyming
word to complete the sentence.

1. | earn | You go to school to _____.

2. | head | You can eat jelly on _____.

3. | steady | It's time to get _____ to go.

4. | leather | We can have a picnic if the _____ is nice.

5. | pearly | The alarm clock rings _____ in the morning.

6. | trickier | The glue is _____ than the tape.

7. | sunniest | We all laughed at the _____ story.

8. | shinier | A fly is tiny, but an ant is _____.

9. | munchy | Crackers are crisp and _____.

10. | learning | My club is _____ money by selling candy.

11. | wealthy | Eat lots of vegetables to stay _____.

12. | grumpier | The pillow is lumpy, but the bed is _____.

Use a word from the box and the prefix below it
to make a new word to complete each sentence.

pack	tie	write	fill

re_____

1. The paper is so messy, I will have to _____ the story.

2. The glass is empty. Will you please _____ it?

3. Ken had to _____ the knot.

4. Jason dropped his backpack. Now he has to _____ it.

like	agree	appear	cover

dis_____

5. The tiny kitten seemed to _____ under the chair.

6. Sue and Pat like carrots, but they _____ spinach.

7. What did you _____ when you lifted the rug?

8. Tim and Steve do not get along. They _____ about everything.

happy	able	plug	load

un_____

9. I saw Kim crying. Why is she so _____?

10. It takes a long time to _____ the boxes from the truck.

11. Turn off the light and _____ the lamp.

12. The little puppy was _____ to go up the steps.

Name

Choose the word from the box that completes each
sentence. Write the word on the line.

1. You throw something away because it is _____.	useful useless
2. A person who does silly things is _____.	foolless foolish
3. Something that can be fixed is _____.	fixable fixless
4. A baby bird cannot take care of itself. It is _____.	helpful helpless
5. The timid puppy is afraid of everything. The puppy is _____.	fearful fearless
6. The girl kept all the candy for herself. She was _____.	selfless selfish
7. Sharon spilled milk and tipped the cereal. She was very _____ this morning.	careful careless
8. The kitten jumped at the yarn and batted it. The kitten was very _____.	playful playing
9. Mr. Smith did not want to spill the water. He lifted the pail very _____.	carelessly carefully
10. That light is very bright. It shines _____.	brightish brightly

Name _____

Read the word and the clue. Choose the prefix or the suffix to add to the word. Write the new word on the line.

Add **re** or **un** at the beginning.

1. tie   What you must do to make a knot disappear   _____

2. pack   What you do to fill your backpack again   _____

3. heat   How to make your dinner warm again   _____

Add **ful** or **less** at the end.

4. help   When you can't help yourself you are   _____

5. sleep   When you cannot go to sleep you are   _____

6. cheer   When you are happy you are   _____

Add **ish** or **less** at the end.

7. fool   To do something that might hurt you is   _____

8. child   When the park has no children, it is   _____

9. self   When people won't share, they are   _____

Add **able** or **ly** at the end.

10. bend   Something you can bend is   _____

11. friend   A person who likes other people is   _____

12. wash   Something that you can wash is   _____

Name

Read the sentences. Then write a word that makes sense in each blank. Use words with the spellings *oo* as in **look**, or *-ould* as in **could**.

Peggy went to the library. She wanted to find a good _____ to read.

"Would you like a book about animals? _____ you like a book about a princess?" asked Mrs. Booker.

"I don't know," said Peggy. "Last week I read about a stuffed panda that could say things. It _____ also sing. It was a _____ story. I am looking for another good story."

"Take your time," said Mrs. _____. "You can keep _____ as long as you want."

At last Peggy saw a _____ that she wanted. But the shelf was too high. She _____ not reach it. Peggy got a little ladder. She _____ on the ladder to get the book. She took the book to check it out.

"Have you read this _____ , Mrs. Booker?" asked Peggy.

Mrs. Booker _____ her head. "Not yet," she said. "Please tell me how you like it."

"I will," said Peggy. Then she _____ the book home.

Write the name of a good book you think Peggy should read.

_____

_____

_____

Choose the word that completes each sentence.
Write the word on the line.

1. If it is part of your body, it must be a _____.	food foot fool
2. If you can read it, it must be a _____.	book boot brook
3. If it's part of a jacket, it must be a _____.	hoot hook hood
4. If you would eat it, it must be _____.	foot food fool
5. If it comes from a tree, it must be _____.	wool woof wood
6. If it's a little stream, it must be a _____.	brook brood booth
7. If you catch fish with it, it must be a _____.	hoop hood hook
8. If thread comes on it, it must be a _____.	spoon spool scoop
9. If it has chocolate chips, it must be a _____.	rookie cookie lookie
10. If it's knitted into a sweater, it must be _____.	wool wood whoosh

Name

Read each set of sentences. Circle the word that is wrong. Then write the correct word on the line.

1. Ms. Baker could not reach the top shelf.
    She got a stool to stand on.
    When she stood on the spoon
    she could reach the shelf.   _____

2. Harry wanted to make breakfast.
    He took out a bowl and a spoon.
    Then he looked for a box of cereal.
    When he shook one box, it was empty.
    The next box he stood was full.   _____

3. Amy went to the brook to fish.
    She had a pole and some worms.
    She put a worm on the hood and
    put it in the water.
    Would a fish bite the hook?   _____

4. Chad had a new cookbook.
    He looked for a good dish to cook.
    He liked meat loaf, but it took too long.
    He would have to look in his cartoon
    for another meal to cook.   _____

5. Dad took Jerry to the zoo.
    Dad likes to look at the lions, and
    Jerry likes to look at the kangaroos.
    They stood near the kangaroo yard.
    They saw a baby stick its head
    out of the lion's pocket.   _____

Read the mixed-up words. Put the words in order
to make a sentence. Write the sentence on the line.
Draw a picture to go with the sentence.

1. down. The fell clown

_____

2. flowers A cow has tail. on its

_____

3. yellow. and owl is The brown

_____

4. flies over of bees crowd A the flower.

_____

Name

Read the word in the box. Then read the sentence.
Change the word in the box to make a new rhyming word
that will complete the sentence.

1. | town | The opposite of *up* is _____.

2. | how | The opposite of *then* is _____.

3. | tower | A gentle rain is a _____.

4. | sound | The opposite of *lost* is _____.

5. | brown | An angry person has a _____ on her face.

6. | how | Do you know that milk comes from a _____?

7. | house | A tiny furry animal is a _____.

8. | loud | You should be _____ of your good work.

9. | scowl | A wolf will _____ at the moon.

10. | dowel | A _____ is useful for drying things.

11. | flower | I'll show you the city from the top of this _____.

12. | pounce | A rubber ball will _____ when you drop it.

13. | shout | Blow the candles _____.

14. | pouch | When you bump your elbow, you say _____!

15. | pound | A circle is a _____ shape.

Name

Read the paragraphs. Then use sentences from the paragraphs to answer the questions.

An owl is a bird that hunts at night. Owls are known to eat little animals and insects. An owl makes hardly any sound when it flies. It may fly low over the ground. Then it swoops down when it has found a mouse or an insect.

How does an owl see at night? It has very big eyes that allow it to see in the dark. But it cannot move its eyes from side to side. It must turn its head to look around.

Most owls are brown or gray. Some baby owls may be gray. They turn brown when they are grown. Snowy owls live in the arctic. They are white to match the snow.

1. Is an owl a loud bird? Write the sentence that tells you.

_____

_____

2. What is strange about an owl's eyes?

_____

_____

3. What color are most owls?

_____

_____

Write the spelling *aw* or *ow* in each blank to complete the words.
Then answer the question. Write the answer on the line.

1. The dog ran until its p_____s were sore.

   It found a nice bed of str_____.

   It lay d_____n to rest.

   Why did the dog rest?

   _____

2. Kim likes to dr_____ and paint.

   Last week she went d_____n to the lake.

   She s_____ swans and fl_____ers.

   What do you think Kim will draw?

   _____

3. The farmer saw crows in the garden.

   He got old clothes and stuffed them with str_____.

   The next morning the crows came at d_____n.

   They squ_____ked and flew away when they saw the str_____ man.

   Why did the crows fly away?

   _____

4. Kenny has a jigs_____ puzzle.

   He dropped a piece d_____n behind the sofa.

   Now he must cr_____l behind the sofa to get it.

   Why must Kenny crawl behind the sofa?

   _____

Use the letters in each box and the word ending below
the box to make a word to complete each sentence.

bec	p	c	appl

____ause

1. The singer likes to hear the _____ of the crowd.

2. I ate a snack _____ I was hungry.

3. To stop for a little while is to _____.

4. The wind will _____ the leaves to fall.

b	th	br	f

____ought

5. Sandy _____ a cake to the picnic.

6. We _____ we knew the answer.

7. Dad _____ a pumpkin from the farmer.

8. The little children _____ over the crayons.

t	c

____aught

9. Our teacher _____ us to do math.

10. The spider _____ a fly in its web.

Name

Choose words from the box to complete each sentence.
Write the words on the lines.

1. The kitten lifts its _____ high when it _____ in wet grass.	paws walks waits
2. Cassandra _____ a new book at the store and _____ it to school.	bought caught brought
3. A _____ is smaller than a _____.	walking basketball walnut
4. A _____ is a person who knows a lot about the _____.	law lawn lawyer
5. We finally _____ the _____ kitten that ran away.	naughty caught awning
6. We wished for an umbrella when we were _____ in the _____ rain.	thoughtful awful caught
7. Mrs. Polly _____ her parrot to _____.	taught tall talk
8. Dennis drew a hopscotch game on the _____with yellow _____.	chalk walnut sidewalk
9. We had to _____ to school _____ our auto would not start.	become because walk

Phonics Review

Name

Read each set of sentences. Circle the word that is
wrong. Then write the correct word on the line.

1. The grass is getting too tall.
   Dad got out the lawn mower.
   He is going to mow the laundry.

   _____

2. I saw my favorite ball player at the mall.
   I was very excited! I wanted his autograph,
   so I asked him to automatic my cap.

   _____

3. Daisy was a naughty dog.
   I heard Mrs. Talbot scold her.
   At first I thought Mrs. Talbot was walking to me!

   _____

4. Our music teacher bought some new music.
   She brought it to school.
   She taught us to sing the songs.
   We like to learn the new songs she tattled us.

   _____

5. We played basketball at the park.
   I almost shot a basket, but I missed.
   I ought to be much better when I grow shorter.

   _____

Choose the right answer to each question.
Write it on the line.

1. Which is royal, a king or a sting? _____

2. What can be corduroy, a shirt or a shrub? _____

3. Which is a toy, a ball gown or a balloon? _____

4. Which herds cattle, a cow bell or a cowboy? _____

5. Which is a trip, a voyage or a village? _____

6. Which is loyal, a pet or a stranger? _____

7. Which means *fun*, enjoyable or joyless? _____

8. Which means *to wreck*, royal or destroy? _____

9. Which is annoying, a good smell or a whining sound? _____

10. Which means *work*, employ or enjoy? _____

11. Is a banging sound enjoying or annoying? _____

12. Which means *happy*, joyful or joyless? _____

13. Who takes a trip, a destroyer or a voyager? _____

14. Which is a person, a toy or a boy? _____

Name

Read the word in the box. Then read the sentence.
Change the word in the box to make a new rhyming
word to complete the sentence.

1. | coin | We want you to _____ our team.

2. | foil | Mark had to heat the water to make

it_____.

3. | choice | Emily has a fine _____ for singing.

4. | joint | I broke the _____ off my pencil.

5. | oil | Some snakes can curl up into a _____.

6. | joins | Nickels, pennies, and dimes are _____.

7. | toil | If you let milk get warm, it could _____.

8. | voice | Dave had to make a _____ between toys or

books.

9. | boil | Dig a well to find _____.

10. | points | Elbows and knees are _____.

11. | foil | In the garden, worms crawl in the _____.

12. | spoiler | Dad cooked the chicken in the _____.

Name

Use the letters in the box to complete the words in the sentences.

oy	ow

1. Bill got a new t_____ car. It has a remote control.

2. He wants to show the b_____s and girls h_____ it works.

ou	oi

3. Last summer, workers f_____nd some _____l in the lake.

4. It could sp_____l the beach.

5. We j_____ned in to help clean it up.

6. I'm pr_____d of the job we did.

ough	ow

7. W_____ ! Mom b_____t a new car.

8. We took it for a ride around t_____n.

9. We th_____t we were cool.

oi	aw

10. Last night we heard a n_____se outside.

11. We looked out at the l_____n.

12. Dad p_____nted to the trash can. It was tipped over.

13. We s_____ a raccoon digging through the trash with its p_____s.

Copyright © 1996 Open Court Publishing Company

Choose words from the box to complete each sentence.
Write the words on the lines.

1. Liz dressed in a clown _____. She wore it to march in a _____.	parade costume perfume
2. Alligators are _____. They live in swampy _____.	reptiles unions regions
3. I hope the picnic will _____ games. One fun game is to sit on a balloon to make it _____.	attitude explode include
4. It's my _____ that the monkeys are the funniest animals at the zoo. They can _____ people.	imitate confusion opinion
5. What did you _____ to do? Should we play games or watch _____?	decide television invade
6. My dog is a good _____. I wouldn't trade him for a _____ dollars.	million decision companion
7. When all the buses _____ at the same time, there is a lot of _____.	confuse arrive confusion
8. If you _____ a balloon too much, it might pop and sound like an _____.	inflate invade explosion

Choose a word from the box to complete each sentence.
Write the word on the line.

1. If it's a day to celebrate, it might be a _____.	birthday Thursday
2. If it's a picture in a book, it's an _____.	illustration illusion
3. If it's a made-up story, it's _____.	action fiction
4. If you want an answer, ask a _____.	quarter question
5. If you don't forget, you _____.	remember register
6. If you go to school, you get an _____.	invasion education
7. If it's a quarrel, it's an _____.	argument article
8. If you go on a trip for fun, it's a _____.	vacant vacation
9. If it makes your skin feel soft, it's _____.	lotion location
10. If it's perfect, it's _____.	personal perfection
11. If he's invited, he has an _____.	invasion invitation
12. If you join me, we are _____.	together tomorrow
13. If it's a part of something, it's a _____.	section session

Read the paragraph. Fill in the blanks with words that make sense. Use words with **-ng** and **-ing**. Then answer the questions.

Look at the tips of your fingers. Do you see tiny, swirling lines? These lines are your _____ prints. The _____ lines make a pattern. The pattern on your _____ is not like the pattern on anyone else's fingers. Your _____ pattern will stay the same as long as you live.

1. What are fingerprints? _____

_____

2. What is special about your fingerprints? _____

_____

3. How long will your fingerprints last? _____

_____

Name _____

Write the sentence on the line.

Draw a picture to go with the sentence.

1. sang together. song We a

_____

2. This ago. dinosaur millions lived of years

_____

3. A is television. reptiles about on show

_____

4. Here party. an invitation to is a birthday

_____

Choose the words that answer each question.
Write the words on the lines.

1. Which can be found in a jungle? _____ _____ _____	tiger dolphin parrot monkey
2. What might you enjoy on a vacation? _____ _____ _____	swimming camping playing excluding
3. What might you use to decorate a wall? _____ _____ _____	lotion painting decoration illustration
4. Which are shapes? _____ _____ _____	rectangle tingle triangle circle
5. What can make a lot of noise? _____ _____ _____	explosion parade howling whispering
6. What can be inside someone's mind? _____ _____ _____	memories lotion imagination opinions

Read each sentence. Choose two words from the box
that mean almost the same thing as the underlined words.
Write the words you choose on the lines.

1. The <u>person</u> had a big <u>meal</u>. _____ _____	diner dinner super sunner
2. The <u>person</u> put <u>raw</u> carrots on the plate. _____ _____	cook cooked cooking uncooked
3. The <u>person</u> thought he was <u>full of luck</u>. _____ _____	winer winner lucky unlucky
4. The baby <u>animal</u> was soft and <u>full of fur</u>. _____ _____	tiger tigger fury furry
5. Adam and Tanya <u>do not agree</u> about how to make the mess <u>get out of sight</u>. _____ _____	disable disagree appear disappear
6. There was a <u>wonderful</u> surprise inside the big <u>box</u>. _____ _____	super supper carton cartoon

Phonics Review

Use the letters in each box and the word ending below
the box to make a word to complete each sentence.
Write the word on the line.

fu	na	pic	crea

_____ture

1. Another word for animal is _____.

2. We saw plants and animals when we hiked along

   the _____ trail.

3. Tina will save her tickets. She may revisit the museum

   in the _____.

4. The sea captain had a _____ of a whale

   on the wall.

fam	danger	curi	humor

_____ous

5. The kitten wants to know what is in the carton.

   The kitten is _____.

6. The actor has made many films. He is _____.

7. Stay away from railroad tracks. They are _____.

8. His story made us laugh. The story was _____.

Name

Choose a word from the box to complete each sentence.
Write the word on the line.

Name

1. If you always want to know what is going on, you are _____.	curious furious cured
2. If a house has a light that warns ships, it is a _____.	lightboat houseboat lighthouse
3. If it is a surprise, it is _____.	expected disrespected unexpected
4. If a storm brings flashing lightning and thunder, it is a _____.	thunderbolt thunderstorm flashlight
5. If you do not find what you hope to find, you might be _____.	appointed disappointed unexpected
6. If flowers grow in nature without anyone caring for them, they grow _____.	nervously needless naturally
7. If you make a fire in it, it is a _____.	fireplace firefighter wildfire
8. If it's an exciting trip, it's an _____.	advertisement adventure appointment
9. If it's absolutely wonderful, it's _____.	fabulous feeble furious